Learning to Read, Step by Step!

Ready to Read   Preschool–K
• big type and easy words • rhyme and rhythm • picture clues
For children who know the alphabet and are eager to begin reading.

Reading with Help   Preschool–Grade 1
• basic vocabulary • short sentences • simple stories
For children who recognize familiar words and sound out new words with help.

Reading on Your Own   Grades 1–3
• engaging characters • easy-to-follow plots • popular topics
For children who are ready to read on their own.

Reading Paragraphs   Grades 2–3
• challenging vocabulary • short paragraphs • exciting stories
For newly independent readers who read simple sentences with confidence.

Ready for Chapters   Grades 2–4
• chapters • longer paragraphs • full-color art
For children who want to take the plunge into chapter books but still like colorful pictures.

STEP INTO READING® is designed to give every child a successful reading experience. The grade levels are only guides; children will progress through the steps at their own speed, developing confidence in their reading. The F&P Text Level on the back cover serves as another tool to help you choose the right book for your child.

Remember, a lifetime love of reading starts with a single step!

For my three beloved children,
Eli, Dafna, and Oren, who have supported
my artistic endeavors and guided me in the
everlasting process of learning the languages
of English, Spanish, and Photoshop
—D.S.

Copyright © 2019 by David Salomon

All rights reserved. Published in the United States by Random House Children's Books, a division of Penguin Random House LLC, New York.

Step into Reading, Random House, and the Random House colophon are registered trademarks of Penguin Random House LLC.

Visit us on the Web!
StepIntoReading.com
rhcbooks.com

Educators and librarians, for a variety of teaching tools, visit us at RHTeachersLibrarians.com

Library of Congress Cataloging-in-Publication Data
Names: Salomon, David, author.
Title: Baby panda goes wild! / by David Salomon.
Description: New York : Random House, [2019] | Series: Step into reading. Step 3
Identifiers: LCCN 2018006193 (print) | LCCN 2018007943 (ebook)
ISBN 978-0-525-57916-8 (trade paperback) | ISBN 978-0-525-57917-5 (hardcover library binding) |
ISBN 978-0-525-57918-2 (ebook)
Subjects: LCSH: Pandas—China—Reintroduction—Juvenile literature. |
Endangered species—Juvenile literature.
Classification: LCC QL795.P18 (ebook) | LCC QL795.P18 S25 2019 (print) |
DDC 599.7890951—dc23

Printed in the United States of America
10 9 8 7 6 5 4 3 2 1

This book has been officially leveled by using the F&P Text Level Gradient™ Leveling System.

STEP INTO READING®

A SCIENCE READER

Baby Panda Goes Wild!

by David Salomon

Random House 🏠 New York

It is dawn

in Sichuan Province, China.

Thick fog covers the mountains.

A baby giant panda wakes up.

The cub is named ChiDa

(say chih-DAH).

She is about five months old

and weighs fifteen pounds.

ChiDa lives at a panda reserve.

In a reserve,

pandas are fed by scientists.

They study panda behavior

and help them breed.

Giant pandas are an
endangered species.
Humans' activities pose
the greatest threat
to the survival of giant pandas.

Other animals do not attack
adult pandas.

The people of China

adore giant pandas.

They are worried that pandas

might become extinct.

Scientists are hard at work
to help the species survive.
Panda survival is very important
to the Chinese people
and their government.

China has over forty reserves,
where the cubs and adults
enjoy comfortable, safe lives.
Growing cubs live in a *kindergarten*.

Giant pandas are bears.

There are eight kinds of bears.

Unlike some of the others,

pandas do not eat meat.

They do not hibernate either.

ChiDa and Mother live in

a walled yard with trees.

Mother was injured in the wild.

People saved her

and moved her to the reserve.

ChiDa wishes Mother would play more and sleep less. Mother either eats or sleeps most of the day and night.

Giant pandas are picky eaters.
Bamboo is nearly their entire diet.
Bamboo contains all the nutrients
giant pandas need.

Bamboo is a plant

in the grass family.

A new shoot of leaves

is the best part to eat.

Adult giant pandas eat

about thirty pounds of bamboo

a day.

Their stomachs absorb

only a small amount

of calories.

The pandas get tired often.

ChiDa cannot eat bamboo yet.
She only drinks
her mother's milk.

ChiDa looks up the tallest tree.

She presses her claws

into the trunk

and pulls herself higher

to hide from Mother.

Mother wakes up.

She chirps and calls ChiDa.

Chirping is a bird-like sound.

ChiDa thinks she has
a good hiding spot.
Surprise!
Mother walks straight
to the tree.

Mother smells ChiDa.

She does not need to look up.

She chirps, and then barks.

ChiDa ignores her.

Mother loses her patience.

She starts to climb the tree.

ChiDa comes down.

Mother wins at hide-and-seek!

ChiDa learns

she cannot hide

from Mother.

Mother weighs about 180 pounds.

Male pandas are bigger
and stronger than females.

Pandas without cubs

prefer to be alone.

Females are ready to mate

only a few days a year.

On those days,

male and female pandas

get together.

It is hard to know when
a panda is pregnant.
The mother does not gain weight.
The cub is born pink and small.
A cub weighs only
four to six ounces at birth.
That's about the weight of a baseball!

Mother is raising ChiDa alone.

Fathers never stay with cubs.

In nature,

most cubs stay with their mothers

for less than two years.

About half the time,

mothers give birth to twins.

In the wild,

it is not possible to feed both.

Usually, only one cub survives.

At the reserve,

scientists have learned

how to raise twin cubs.

It used to be rare
for panda cubs
to be born in captivity,
which means being raised
by people.
But this has changed.
In 2015,
thirty-five cubs were born
on Chinese reserves.

ChiDa is now eight months old.

She eats bamboo.

She and Mother are moved

to a bamboo forest

with a fence around it.

ChiDa is chosen

to be released into the wild.

This is part of

an important program.

Its goal is to increase

the number of pandas

in the wild.

First the scientists want
ChiDa to learn all she can
from Mother.
This will help ChiDa
survive by herself
after Mother leaves.

Mother is moved back
to the original reserve.
At twenty months old,
ChiDa is now alone.
The scientists wear
panda suits.
They teach ChiDa how
to survive in the wild.

Most likely,
fewer than 1,900
giant pandas
live in the wild today.
People move into the
pandas' natural habitat.
They cut bamboo
and build roads.
Pandas are forced into
areas with less food.

Eating bamboo
limits where pandas can live.
Today wild giant pandas
are only in central China.

Only half of the giant pandas
that are released survive.
Adjusting to life in the wild
is very difficult.

In the wild,

the giant panda defends its area.

It fights any other panda

who dares enter its territory.

ChiDa is now

thirty months old.

She weighs as much as Mother.

Scientists move her

nearer to the giant pandas'

natural habitat.

She finds all the bamboo

she needs.

ChiDa's training gets harder.
The scientists teach her about
the danger of stepping into
another panda's territory.

Scientists fit ChiDa
with a collar that has
a GPS transmitter.
GPS stands for
Global Positioning System.
The GPS connects to satellites.
It sends information about
ChiDa's location.

Today is her big day!
ChiDa is released
into the wild bamboo forest
near Wolong.